Explaining
Trust

Tom Marshall

Sovereign World

Unless otherwise stated,
all Bible quotations are from the *New International Version*.
Copyright © 1973, 1978, International Bible Society,
published by Hodder and Stoughton.

ISBN: 1-85240-078-1

Production & Printing in England for
SOVEREIGN WORLD LIMITED
P.O. Box 17, Chichester, West Sussex PO20 6YB
by Nuprint Ltd, Station Road, Harpenden, Herts AL5 4SE.

Contents

Introduction:
The Importance Of Trust

Trust is essential to any life in society since social interaction and social organisation would be impossible in a world where nobody could be trusted. We need a dependable and predictable environment to be able to order our life with reasonable confidence, therefore we desire the world, and people in it to be trustworthy.

We come into this world trusting. Suspicion and mistrust are things we learn later and they are always painful experiences. They change the innocent eyes of childhood into the wary, watchful eyes that look out of so many faces.

Trust is a necessary condition for the formation of any type of personal relationship. Can you imagine someone saying to you, 'I would really like to be your friend, but remember of course, I don't trust you.' Your reply would probably be 'Go find yourself another friend.'

The more important the relationship is, the more vital is the part played by trust. If I am part of a climbing team and hanging over a cliff on the end of a rope, the primary concern in my mind regarding the man on the other end of the rope is not whether I like him, but whether I can trust him. My life may depend on that.

The more intimate the relationship is, the more costly the commitment of trust becomes, thus it lies right at the heart of relationships like marriage or leadership.

Because all relationships involve trust, it is necessarily involved in our relationship with God because we relate to

God in exactly the same way as we relate to other people. That is why faith is not a condition that God has capriciously laid down; the strangest thing would be to discover that it was possible to have a personal relationship with God that did not involve trust.

But what is it?

Although trust is so essential, its nature and its requirements are by no means well known. In the Church we call it faith and publish hundreds of books every year to extol its virtues, praise its achievements and try to explain its dynamics. It, or more of it, is widely regarded as the answer to all of our problems and the key to health, happiness, prosperity, success, fruitfulness and spiritual maturity. But acquiring it, or developing it remains to most Christians a tantalising mystery.

It is therefore worth our while to get some clarity on what trust or faith really is, before we get too far in our discussion of its role in personal relationships. To do so we will have to get behind or beyond the slogans, religious or otherwise, such as 'Have faith', 'Trust me', 'Only believe' and so on.

What is trust? What are its conditions? What happens when you trust? How do you build trust? How is trust broken or lost? When it is lost, can it be restored? These are basic but vital questions whose answers we cannot assume or take for granted as being common knowledge. Some of the answers you will find in the following pages.

1

The Nature Of Trust

We will begin by attempting a simple definition of the nature
of interpersonal trust—

> To trust someone is to voluntarily make yourself
> dependent on that person for some outcome or other,
> or for some result or consequence.

Note the following very important characteristics that
describe the situation we have defined as trust.

Trust is a choice we make

Trust or faith cannot be forced on us, if we are going to trust
someone or put our faith in them we must do it voluntarily.
If people are told by their leaders, 'You will just have to
trust us in this,' the one thing you can be sure of is that they
won't trust them even if control of the outcome is out of the
people's hands and they have no option but to leave it in the
hands of the leaders.

Trust is an attitude

Attitudes are what govern our life and behaviour. Attitudes
are different from beliefs because beliefs are purely cogni-

tive and we do not generally act on our beliefs. Trust as an attitude has three components,

a. A Cognitive element, that is we are convinced that the other person is trustworthy. Abraham was

> *fully persuaded that God had power to do what he had*
> *promised.* (Romans 4:21)

b. An emotional element, that is we feel confident about trusting the other person.

> *Faith is being sure of what we hope for and certain of*
> *what we do not see.* (Hebrews 11:1)

c. A volitional element, that is we act on it. Like Peter we have to get out of the boat and walk on water (Matthew 14:29).

> *Faith without deeds is useless.* (James 2:20)

To be trusted is a responsibility we voluntarily accept

You cannot expect someone to be trustworthy unless they know and accept the terms of that trust and the responsibility of faithfulness. In other words there is a mutuality about it. Conscious and deliberate trust on one side has to be matched by conscious and deliberate trustworthiness on the other; conscious and deliberate faith on one side has to be matched by conscious and deliberate faithfulness on the other.

The trusting person must also himself be trustworthy

A little reflection will reveal why this must be so.

a. For me to be able to trust requires that the person I trust be trustworthy, that is he takes seriously his obligation to be reliable and faithful to me.

b. But a person is unlikely to take on such serious and possibly onerous obligations towards me if he discovers that I for my part do not take such obligations seriously at all.

c. Moreover, if I do not take trustworthiness seriously in my own behaviour I will find it very hard to believe that anyone else will do so and therefore I will have great difficulty in trusting anybody.

The one who would trust must be one who is trustworthy.

The one who would have faith must be one who is faithful.

Trust is a risk we take

When we trust we let some of the outcomes of our life go out of our sole control and partly or completely into the control of someone else, on whose faithfulness and ability we have chosen to rely. We cannot trust someone to do something and then do it all ourselves. That may get the thing done but it makes nonsense of our claim to trust.

Vulnerability is the cost of trust

To trust always involves us taking a position of vulnerability because we no longer have sole control over our lives. This is always a costly step, emotionally and psychologically, even if in no other way. There is no such thing as costless trust.

Because of this we will always find it easier to expect other people to trust us than for us to trust other people, for other people to be committed to us than for us to be committed to other people. This is the almost perennial failure on the part of many Christian leaders.

The proof that we have trusted is that we make no contingency plans in case the other person lets us down

If we set up a fall-back position or 'hedge our bets' or provide against a possible let down, it may be admirable discretion but it certainly calls into question the level of our trust. If the other person learns of our contingency plans they will soon realise that we don't really trust them at all.

To accept trust involves accountability

If I am trusted, and I have accepted that trust, I am answerable for the outcome, whatever it is, and have to explain any failure. That is why some people avoid positions of trust that are also positions of responsibility, because they do not want to be held accountable for results.

Because trust involves vulnerability, strong emotions are always aroused when trust is broken

There is generally a lot of anger and hostility towards the person guilty of breaking trust but the root of such anger is fear because our supposedly predictable universe is suddenly seen to be unreliable and undependable. This generates anxiety. We think, 'If you can't trust a person like that, who on earth can you trust?'

Trust once broken is very difficult to restore

Trust differs from other virtues in its extreme fragility. Once trust is broken it is very, very difficult to restore. A person may act unlovingly on one occasion but we will still believe that they are essentially loving, they may do us an unkindness and we will still believe that they are really kindly by nature. But if we trust someone and they let us down, we are likely to have a question mark about their trustworthiness for a long time to come. The reason for this has something to do with the all-or-nothing nature of trust and also with the state of vulnerability that trust creates.

Firstly when it comes to trust, you either do or you don't. You cannot partially trust, or if you do the uncertainty created causes extreme discomfort. Trust is like commitment—yes or no, in or out, and when it is broken it is never partially broken, if it is broken at all it is totally broken.

Secondly in trust we are in a position of vulnerability in that we have chosen to rely on someone else, and if they fail us there is a strong emotional let down that is very painful.

Like a bad tooth and an unsteady foot is confidence in a faithless man in time of trouble. (Proverbs 25:19, ASB)

Love is far more rugged and enduring than trust and can survive long after trust is lost. This creates enormous vulnerability. A person who is bound by love to a partner who they can no longer trust is exposed to the possibility of intense hurt.

The restoration of trust, where trust has been lost, always takes time. Forgiveness for the breach of trust can be the work of a moment but the restoration of confidence and the willingness to again take the risk of trusting is not the work of a moment, it may need patient rebuilding.

For this reason trust needs to be guarded very carefully and the need to be trustworthy taken very seriously.

It is required that those who have been given a trust must prove faithful. (1 Corinthians 4:2)

Why do we find it hard to trust?

Some of the reasons why we seem to find trust or faith difficult may already have emerged from what we have already discussed.

1. We do not understand the terms of trust,
for example,

a. Trust depends on relationships. You cannot safely trust somebody you do not know or whose character or capabilities are unknown. To do so might be a dangerous presumption.

They [the sheep] *will never follow a stranger; in fact, they will run away from him because they do not recognise a stranger's voice.* (John 10:5)

b. The basis of trust and the scope of trust must be mutually known and agreed by both parties. We need to know, not only who we can trust, but what we can trust them for. To know and trust the integrity and honesty of a person does not necessarily mean that we can trust their advice on medical or financial matters. Thus the basis of our trust in God is expressed in His trust deed, His covenants, in which He makes known not only His faithful character but also the precise terms on which He offers His gracious proposals to His creatures. Trust, like faith, is never a leap in the dark, it rests on knowledge.

2. Past hurts and disappointments may have made us wary and cautious.

We may have trusted in the past and been badly let down so that we are afraid of being hurt again. Or we may ourselves have been guilty of breaking trust and are afraid of further failure. What we have experienced is the fallenness of a world that having broken faith with God now weighs heavily against trustworthiness or faithfulness in all its manifestations.

> *Many a man claims to have unfailing love,*
> *But a faithful man who can find?* (Proverbs 20:6)

3. In trusting we come up against the root of our own fallenness.

The root of that fallenness is the rebellious refusal of our creaturely dependence on God the Creator. Instead we have chosen to strive to

- a. Be independent,
- b. Seek self sufficiency, and
- c. Exercise sole control over our own destiny.

Trust strikes at the root of all three of these motivations therefore it meets resistance from all of them.

Trust means that instead of independence I have to settle for interdependence, to be dependent on others in relationships and to allow others to depend on me.

Instead of self sufficiency I recognise my incompleteness without others and instead of total autonomy, I allow the control of certain outcomes in my life to go out of my hands into the hands of other people.

2

The Content Of Trust

To increase our understanding of trust and trustworthiness we will examine some of the terms, qualities and character traits that surround and help to give it content and substance.

Confidence

Confidence is heart trust, it is trust that has been proved right so often that it has come to a state of settled conviction or assurance regardless of what the issue is. The repeated acts of trust have produced a state or condition of confidence.

> *Because God has said, 'Never will I leave you, never will I forsake you.' So we say with confidence 'The Lord is my helper; I will not be afraid. What can man do to me?'*
> (Hebrews 13:6)

So also Paul writes to the Corinthians:

> *I have great confidence in you; I take great pride in you. I am greatly encouraged.* (2 Corinthians 7:4)

Confidence is essential for intimacy. We confide only in those we can trust, therefore trust lies at the heart of the most intimate of our relationships.

A wife of noble character who can find? She is worth far more than rubies. Her husband has full confidence in her and lacks nothing of value. (Proverbs 31:10–11)

The Lord confides in those who fear him; he makes his covenant known to them. (Psalm 25:14)

Loyalty

Loyalty is faithfulness at its most personal and most committed. It says,

    a. 'I will be here in the bad times as well as the good.'
    b. 'I will be for you even when everyone else is against you.'
    c. 'I will defend you, even at cost or risk to myself.'

Loyalty is an essential component of the most important and most intimate of our relationships. We rightly despise the 'fair weather friend' or those who desert commitments because the going gets rough.

A friend loves at all times, and a brother is born for adversity. (Proverbs 17:17)

Reliability and dependability

To be able to trust someone requires that we can rely on them or depend on them to do what they have undertaken to do without the need for us to check up on them to see whether it is being done or not.

Reliability and dependability are built up by faithfulness in small things and these small things often have a symbolic significance far beyond their immediate importance.

The first one came and said; 'Sir, your mina has earned ten more.' 'Well done, my good servant' the master replied. 'Because you have been trustworthy in a very small matter, take charge of ten cities'. (Luke 19:16–17)

On the other hand, if a person is unreliable in small things, the judgement is likely to be, 'If you cannot trust him in little things, what will he be like if we strike a real crisis?'

Consistency

To be able to trust someone we need predictable responses on their part. How can you trust someone who today is wildly enthusiastic about a project and tomorrow couldn't care less, or who one day treats something as a great joke and the next day gets furiously angry about it.

Similarly it is difficult to trust the very impulsive person because you are never very sure what he or she will do or whether they will leap into action on very inadequate consideration or information.

Consistency requires that we live by principles and not by moods and that we act, not on whim or impulse but on the basis of a rational or sensible consideration of the facts of the situation.

Faithfulness and promise keeping

This is dependability of word, keeping promises or vows even when it is inconvenient or costly to do so.

Today the importance of keeping promises has almost disappeared from sight, and the modern promise appears to have an unexpressed proviso, 'Provided it is still convenient and my feelings haven't changed or circumstances haven't changed, I promise...'. With such conditional promises, it is no wonder that people's commitment also tends to be conditional. How can you commit yourself unreservedly to someone who may back out of their undertakings if something better turns up?

Our ability to trust the Word of God rests on two very important truths.

1. God never changes. He says,

I the Lord do not change. (Malachi 3:6)

Jesus Christ is the same yesterday and today and for ever. (Hebrews 13:8)

2. Because God never changes, His word never changes.

I will not violate my covenant or alter what my lips have uttered. (Psalm 89:34)

Forever, O Lord, thy word is settled in heaven. (Psalm 119:89, ASB)

Honesty and truth speaking

It is very difficult to trust someone when you cannot depend on them to tell the truth or when you suspect that they are deceiving you.

A truthful witness gives honest testimony, but a false witness tells lies. (Proverbs 12:17)

But trust is also made difficult by the following ways of communicating that we sometimes do not recognise as also being deceptive, or giving the impression of being deceptive.

1. Telling less than the whole truth. What we say is true but it does not give the whole picture.

2. Speaking indirectly. This is very common. We do not

say it the way it is but do it obliquely or by inference so that the person will 'know what we mean', or 'know what we are getting at.'

It is very difficult to trust a statement that has a hidden agenda or leaves us trying to 'read between the lines.'

3. Communicating the facts but not our feelings so that the other person is left guessing about how we really view the matter.

Things that breach trust or make trust difficult

The ways that trust can be broken are as diverse as the ways in which trust is placed but the following failures are particularly damaging and embrace most of the typical situations that arise.

1. Breach of confidence
'You let others know.'

If we open our heart to someone in confidence and then find what we have shared is common knowledge it will be a long time before we take that kind of a risk again. Confidences are generally matters of intimacy and disclosure is very hurtful.

> *A gossip betrays a confidence but a trustworthy man keeps a secret.* (Proverbs 11:13)

2. Disloyalty
'You took sides against me', or 'when things got bad you weren't there as you promised.'

Disloyalty is particularly devastating because it occurs at times of critical vulnerability and exposure. When we most need the person's support it is not there or it has even joined forces with those who are against us.

3. Betrayal
'You sacrificed my trust for your own personal gain.'

The difference between disloyalty and betrayal is that the disloyal person deserts his friends, the betrayer is a traitor. Peter denied Jesus, that was disloyalty; Judas did it for money, that was betrayal.

> *Even my close friend in whom I trusted, he who shared my bread, has lifted up his heel against me.*
>
> (Psalm 41:19)

4. Unfaithfulness
'You broke your promise or your vows.'

When we make a promise we voluntarily put certain restrictions on our freedom of action to do, or not to do certain things. What is more, we affirm or confirm our commitment in a deliberate way that is meant to be taken seriously, and relied on by the person to whom we make the promise. The assumption is that we will feel 'bound' to keep our pledge and that the other person can trust us to do so. When we break our word we devastate trust.

> *They make many promises, take false oaths and make agreements; therefore lawsuits spring up like poisonous weeds in a ploughed field.* (Hosea 10:4)

Dishonesty
'I can't believe what you say.'

God is a God of truth and that truth is expressed in his Son Jesus Christ, the Word. Truth, word and faith are linked together. Satan is a liar and the father of lies (John 8:44). The devil, lies and mistrust go together. Lies and dishonesty are parasitic, they succeed only because they deceive people into trusting them as the truth.

Moral weakness

'I leaned on you for support and you gave way under me.'

When, in times of crisis, people who we think are strong, and on whom we rely for support collapse under us we feel particularly exposed and defenceless.

> *You are depending on Egypt, that splintered reed of a staff, which pierces a man's hand and wounds him if he leans on it!*
> (Isaiah 36:6)

Uncertainty and indecisiveness

'You can't make up your mind.'

When we trust we are seeking some degree of certainty, and look for it either in the character, the ability or the resources of the person we are hoping to be able to rely on. If we find that person doubtful, hesitant or vacillating, we will soon conclude that certainty is unlikely to be found there.

Unreliability and inconsistency

'I can't depend on you.'

Moodiness and emotional instability

'I'm not sure you'll feel the same way next time.'

To be able to trust someone requires that their behavioural and emotional responses are predictable, that the way that they are likely to behave and respond in the future will be consistent with the way we have seen them respond in the past. Inconsistency and moodiness, which is emotional inconsistency, makes such prediction difficult.

Lack of self confidence

'How can I be sure of you when you are not sure of yourself?'

This is particularly important where the people concerned are leaders, fathers, husbands and authority figures. We are

21

unlikely to place much reliance on the judgement or support of someone, *'Whose confidence is fragile, and whose trust a spider's web'* (Job 8:14).

Unfairness or injustice
'I can't rely on getting a fair deal.'

Where a person's responses or reactions are affected or influenced by partiality, favouritism, discrimination, prejudice, dogmatism or other distortions, we can have little confidence in their decisions because we never know the hidden agenda on which they have been based.

Carelessness or thoughtlessness
'You mind is not on what you are doing.'

The person who is careless or thoughtless will let people down, not through deliberate intent but through neglect. It is the classic sin of omission as far as trust is concerned because to trust someone I need to be sure that they care about the concerns which I entrust to them, and will take thought about discharging the responsibilities they have accepted.

3

Trust—Crisis Or Process?

Trust, like faith which means the same thing, can be both a crisis and a process, a decision and something that emerges and develops gradually over time. We need to understand both aspects.

Trust as a decision

In any situation which has the potential for a relationship to emerge, there is a period of tentative exploration, investigation and experimentation to see if the relationship will work. During that period changes of mind, wavering and hesitancy are perfectly permissible. But eventually there comes a point of decision when the question of ongoing trust has to be settled one way or another.

A courtship is one example. There may be bursts of enraptured enthusiasm for the only beloved, interspersed with agonised questionings and fears that it is all a horrible mistake. But eventually it has to be settled, 'Yes' or 'No', In or Out. A person knows when the die is cast and the trust commitment made. To change one's mind or to revert to uncertainty after that point is already disloyalty.

The same is true with an employer hiring an accountant. He may vacillate between Smith, Brown and McTavish as being the best man for this position of trust, and change his mind six times a day if he wants to, even to the extent of rejecting them all. But once he decides on McTavish and gives him the job he faces possible legal action if he decides after all he doesn't trust him and wants to sack him.

In voluntary organisations such as a church, having the position of formal authority in leadership does not necessarily mean that you have the trust of all the people. When new leaders take over there is also a time of uncertainty when people are making up their minds as to whether they can put their trust in them. But sooner or later a time for decision has to come and unless the leaders know that they have the trust of the people, they may be able to maintain things in being but they will never be able to lead the church anywhere.

Trust as a process

But trust is also a process—trust has to grow. One act of trust is not enough to provide it with enough impetus to survive the rigours of a relationship. The New Testament gives far more attention to the growth and building up of faith after we have come to Christ than it does to the initial act of faith that puts us into Christ.

This is arguably the biggest lack in teaching on marriage skills. There is a lot of attention to building love and building understanding but very little on how to build trust or how to develop trustworthiness. If we gave it the on-going attention and care it deserves, we would almost certainly have far fewer marriages foundering on broken vows and broken promises.

How to build trust

1. Building our trust in the other person and building their trustworthiness.

We have already seen that trust and trustworthiness go together, so that increasing our capacity to trust, is also dependent on increasing the other person's trustworthiness. Here are the important steps.

a. Remember that you have to take risks. There is no such thing as costless trust and the cost is the vulnerability that is inevitable if we let real outcomes go out of our hands into the hands of another person.

Sometimes we say that trust has to be earned and there is a certain truth in that. But it is also true to say that I cannot prove that I can be trusted unless someone is prepared to take the risk of trusting me. That is the point of the parable of the minas or talents, in Luke 19. The nobleman's servants could prove their faithfulness or trustworthiness only because the nobleman entrusted them with his money.

b. When trusting, play to the person's strengths not their weaknesses, that is, trust them in the beginning with things that they are good at and they like doing. This is very important for parents bringing their children up to be trust-worthy people.

c. Be prompt to praise success and express your confidence in them. To be trusted is honouring and to be recognised as trustworthy is a very rewarding experience.

> *Well done, good and faithful servant! You have been faithful with a few things; I will put you in charge of many things! Come and share your master's happiness.*
> (Matthew 25:23)

d. Model faithfulness and trustworthiness in your own behaviour and character. Children particularly, learn by modelling and they will prize trustworthiness as a virtue only when they see it practised by those they admire most, that is, their parents.

e. Let their success lead on to greater responsibility but be sure to do it in small steps. The rule is line upon line, line upon line, a little here, a little there (Isaiah 28:13). Be patient, remember you are building trust, not finding out how far you can trust or testing its limits. Therefore do not stretch your own or the other person's capacity too far too fast.

f. If the person fails you, give them another chance to succeed. Go back to where they succeeded last time and start again. And even when the person fails *be very cautious about saying, 'I trusted you and you let me down.'* This is particularly important as far as children are concerned, and the reason is that trust is such a fragile thread at the beginning, that if you tell a person that you don't trust them it will be a long time before they can believe your later assurances that now you do trust them.

g. If you are really testing someone or trying them out, do not say that you are trusting them. There is a proper place for trying a person out but it is not the same as trusting. If my boss says to me, 'I'm trying you out to see if you can do this job' and I fail, all that we have found out is that I am unable to do the job. But if he says, 'I am trusting you to do this job well' and then I fail, I have shown that I am untrustworthy.

h. Never say to a child, or to anyone else, 'I trusted you and you have let me down' if they didn't know beforehand that they were on trust and had accepted the trust placed in them.

2. Building the other person's trust in our trustworthiness
Trustworthiness is built in very unspectacular ways, with very little panache and flair, therefore it is more difficult for

some temperaments than others, not because it is hard but because it is painstaking. Here is what you need to do:

a. Create a climate of trustworthiness and dependability, particularly;

i. Be reliable and conscientious in discharging responsibilities and fulfilling tasks or obligations.

ii. Keep promises, even when it is inconvenient and irksome or costly to do so.

iii. Be consistent, act out of principle not on whims or impulse.

iv. Be meticulous in keeping confidence, but never promise confidentiality without knowing first what it is all about.

b. Be honest, share your feelings as well as your thoughts so that there are no inferences to be made or hidden agendas to create suspicion.

c. Work at your character. Remember that a crisis does not create character it only shows the character that is already there.

i. Know yourself and the weaknesses that have to be guarded against or strengthened.

ii. Don't allow yourself to take the soft options or the easy way out. The right way is generally the more difficult of the options.

iii. Never compromise your principles under pressure or for the sake of expediency.

d. Take your responsibilities seriously and what you do, do with all your might (Ecclesiastes 9:10).

e. Be cheerful and avoid complaining in the bad times or falling into self pity when the going gets rough. It is extraordinarily difficult to have confidence in someone who is always sorry for themselves.

4

Restoring Broken Trust

We have emphasised already that trust is very fragile, and once broken or lost is very difficult to restore, if indeed sometimes it can ever be restored apart from the grace of God.

The restoration of trust is a serious matter, therefore every breach of trust must be treated as a grave offence, even in what may seem to be minor matters. One of the main reasons why trust is so difficult to restore is that it is not taken seriously enough, as though, if I break trust, an apology and a promise to do better next time is all that is needed to reinstate me as a person who can be trusted.

The process of restoration involves four stages, none of which can be overlooked.

1. Repentance
2. Restitution
3. Redemption
4. Reordering

Repentance

Repentance is more than an apology or an expression of regret for what has happened. It requires a clear understanding by the offender of what has actually occurred and what is to be done about it.

For true repentance there has to be:

1. A sincere acknowledgement that:

    a. A law of God has been broken.
    b. It is a righteous law, and
    c. It was wrong to break it.

The law that has been broken is that of truth or faithfulness. To break it is an offence against the character of God who is the Faithful and True (Revelation 19:11) and whose word is that which is trustworthy and true (Revelation 21:5).

2. A sincere acknowledgement of personal guilt, without excuse or rationalisation.
Rationalisation is finding a reason for our behaviour that is not the real reason but is one that is more comfortable for our ego to live with.

3. A sincere intention to amend and to be obedient in future to the law that has been broken.

4. Faith that the offended party;

    a. Is willing to forgive,
    b. Forgives, not only as one who has suffered personal injury but forgives as one who righteously resents the offence committed against the law of God.

This is extremely important. For the wrongdoing to be adequately dealt with, the offender not only has to offer sincere repentance but must be able to believe that the one who forgives still preserves a high regard for the law that has been broken. Forgiveness must be taken as seriously as repentance, and must not be dismissed with, 'Never mind, it doesn't matter.'

Restitution

This is of vital importance, not to the question of forgiveness as such, but to the matter of restoration. The key passage is Leviticus 6:2–6, which provides that if a person deceives his neighbour about something entrusted to him, or if he cheats him or swears falsely;

1. He must return what was entrusted to him or whatever he swore falsely about,

2. He must make restitution in full, add a fifth in value to it and return it to the owner,

3. He must bring a guilt offering for the priest to make atonement for him.

Restitution is not earning forgiveness, it is making amends or reparation for the wrong that has been done. It may involve a public apology if the breach of trust has affected a body of people, or it may involve some voluntary service for the person who has been let down, or the voluntary giving up of certain freedoms or interests to give more time to a wife who has been deceived by marital unfaithfulness.

The purpose is neither punishment nor earning forgiveness, it is the restoration of relationships. Therefore the form that restitution takes should arise out of a mutual agreement between the parties as to what is appropriate under the circumstances.

Redemption

The only place where we can find a resource that is able to restore trust is the place which alone has the resource that can provide forgiveness, that is the Cross of Jesus Christ.

1. The death of Jesus was the ultimate expression of forgiveness.

> *But Jesus was saying, 'Father forgive them; for they do not know what they are doing'.* (Luke 23:34, ASB)

Therefore, not only does the Cross secure our forgiveness, it also makes available the grace for us to be forgiving.

> *Be kind and compassionate to one another, forgiving each other, just as in Christ God forgave you.*
> (Ephesians 4:32)

2. The death of Jesus was also the ultimate expression of human trust. On the Cross he let the outcome of his very life and eternal destiny go out of his hands into the hands of the Father. He not only said *'I will put my trust in him'* (Hebrews 2:13), He did it,

> *Jesus called out with a loud voice, 'Father into your hands I commit my spirit.' When he had said this he breathed his last.* (Luke 23:46)

Because of this there is at the Cross a divine resource of trust, injected into the bloodstream of humanity that

a. Can give a person the confidence to trust again after trust has been lost beyond recovery, and

b. Can give the capacity to be trustworthy again after a person has lost all confidence in his ability to be worthy of trust.

Just as forgiveness, and the ability to forgive, is a supernatural gift of grace and is received by faith at the Cross of Jesus Christ, so the redemption of trust, the willingness and the ability to trust again after trust has been repeatedly broken, is also a supernatural gift of grace, likewise received by faith.

In the same way, the faithfulness that can make an habitually untrustworthy person trustworthy, is a supernatural renewal that is received by faith.

Just as salvation makes a rebellious person obedient, an impure person pure, and an habitual liar honest, it makes the unfaithful and disloyal person able to be trusted and worthy of trust.

But something has been added. Now our trustworthiness is guarded by someone we can depend upon, the One who is the Faithful and True.

> *I know whom I have believed and am convinced that he is able to guard what I have entrusted to him.*
> (2 Timothy 1:12)

Reordering

Another vital aspect of restoration, that is too often neglected, is the willingness to spend time rebuilding the areas of our life that have proved to be flawed. This is the work of sanctification that follows the act of faith in redemption. Deliberate discipline is necessary even though it is often a painful process to go through.

> *No discipline seems pleasant at the time, but painful. Later on however, it produces a harvest of righteousness and peace for those who have been trained by it.*
> (Hebrews 12:11)

Often it is helpful to have a mentor, a spiritual friend who can be both compassionate and objective and who can help the person to see through some of the unconscious defence mechanisms that blind them to the truth.

The specific situation needs to be carefully examined to discover or decide, as accurately as possible, the following issues:

1. What is the nature of the failure? What happened?

There may be one major and obvious breach of trust that has brought disaster or it may be a tangled skein of dishonesties, evasions, deceits and broken promises that need to be patiently unravelled to establish the facts. Often there is a great deal of confusion in the mind of the offender that makes it impossible for him to see the issues with any degree of clarity.

2. What is the cause of the failure? Why did it happen?

This requires even greater care and insight because we are probing causation. Is the person afraid to commit himself, and if so why? Does he get into difficult situations through thoughtlessness or carelessness and then seek the easiest way out? Does the failure show up character flaws that need to be addressed, for example, problems with lust, anger or untruthfulness? Does the person have an inordinate desire to be accepted, or loved, or admired?

The aim is to enable the person to understand the problems that have to be faced but also to have the courage to face them with the confidence that they can be overcome.

3. How can the cause or causes of failure be corrected?

This means developing specific strategies to enable dangerous or unhelpful patterns of behaviour to be discarded and more consistent and helpful patterns to be learned in their place.

Or it may be that ministry is needed for emotional or inner healing or to break bondages or ties whose existence has been discovered.

The essential thing is to go beyond understanding the nature of the problem, and to begin to take remedial action.

At the same time that the remedial work is under way, steps also need to be taken to build trust as described in chapter 3.

4. How can we know that the weakness or failure has been overcome?

Time is needed, not only for the person's commitment to the prescribed courses of action to take effect, but also for the dealings of God in his or her life.

Encouragement is also necessary though, and recognition of the progress being made until the person functions with growing confidence in the areas where they have failed before.

Restoring the person whose capacity to trust has been damaged

A person who has trusted but has been let down badly and often, may eventually be so hurt and damaged that they find it impossible to trust anybody again.

> *I believed; therefore I said 'I am greatly afflicted.' And in my dismay I said, 'All men are liars'.* (Psalm 116:11)

> *...a wife deserted and distressed in spirit—a wife who married young only to be rejected.* (Isaiah 54:6)

For such people, the grace of God that enables them to begin to trust again may need to be accompanied by;

1. Healing of the wounds in the human spirit and the emotions.

a. It is essential for the person to forgive the one who has sinned against them and to let go all resentment and bitterness. If I hold on to bitter feelings I effectively lock Christ out because he cannot heal me if by so doing he would seem to justify me in my bitter feelings.

b. It is important for the person to realise that Jesus knows what it feels like to have his trust disappointed. His disciples abandoned him and one of them betrayed him. But because he suffered to the uttermost in all these ways he is able to heal us to the uttermost.

c. Healing needs to be ministered in the power of the Spirit. The Holy Spirit is the one who can take the healing that flows from the Cross and bind up our broken hearts.

> *The Spirit of the Sovereign Lord is on me, because the Lord has anointed me to preach good news to the poor. He has sent me to bind up the broken hearted.*
>
> (Isaiah 61:1)

2. An examination of the reasons for the broken trust.

It is essential to probe the circumstances surrounding the broken trust as there may be important lessons to be learned from the situation, or there may be moral or spiritual issues that may have to be dealt with, for example:

a. Was trust placed presumptuously or foolishly? For example was it done without knowing the character of the person who was trusted or ignoring clear warning signals?

b. Was trust placed for the wrong or self centred reasons? Was it to secure personal advantage or as part of a relationship that itself was wrong?

c. Was the trust itself idolatrous, that is, was it trusting a person for things that we are meant to trust God for, for example for unconditional unchanging love and acceptance? If this is so, the fault not that of the person who failed to give what only God can give.

3. An encouragement of the person's trust in God.

The person's ability and willingness to trust God needs to be encouraged and reinforced. This is the rock beneath our feet. When we put our trust in him, he will never fail us. The most bruised and broken heart can find refuge in him.

> *To you O Lord I lift up my soul;*
>   *in you I trust O my God*
> *No-one whose hope is in you*
>   *will ever be put to shame.*   (Psalm 25:1–2)

> *In God I trust; I will not be afraid.*
> *What can mortal men do to me?*   (Psalm 56:4)

4. The participation of someone trustworthy so that the damaged person can safely venture to begin to trust again.

The rules in chapter 3 for building trust also apply here, but note particularly the following:

a. Start small, the first steps need to be tentative but safe.

b. Give the person time to be comfortable with the measure of trust they have been able to give. Let them set the pace.

c. Build little by little, don't go too far too fast.

d. Reinforce every successful step taken, and give encouragement if they fail at any time. Start all over again.

e. Return their trust. The person receiving trust has to be seen as taking the same risks with them as they are taking with that person.

5

Trust And Faith

Trust and faith are very closely related, in fact, trust may be said to be an aspect of faith. But trust also has some special characteristics that help to illustrate the nature of our relationship with God.

1. We relate to God in the same way as we relate to other people.

This means that when we trust God we let the outcome of the whole of our life, including our eternal destiny, go out of our hands into God's hands. It is a choice we make and the proof that we have made it is that we make no contingency plans in case God lets us down.

2. Trust has a basis that rests on knowledge.

Trust with God as its object is never a leap in the dark, it rests on our knowledge of

a. God's character (often referred to as His name), in particular His faithfulness, truth and love.

b. God's ways or His deeds, the consistent ways in which God works, and

c. God's word, the revelation of His will and purposes.

Those who know your name will trust in you, for you,

Lord, have never forsaken those who seek you.
(Psalm 9:10)

But I am like an olive tree flourishing in the house of God; I trust in God's unfailing love for ever and ever.
(Psalm 52:8)

Trust in the Lord forever, for the Lord, the Lord is the Rock eternal.
(Isaiah 26:4)

In awesome deeds thou dost answer us O God of our salvation, thou who art the trust of all the ends of the earth and of the farthest sea.
(Psalm 65:5, ASB)

Here is a trustworthy saying that deserves full acceptance; Christ Jesus came into the world to save sinners.
(1 Timothy 1:15)

3. How to develop trust
Because trust has a basis in our knowledge of God, it is developed by:

a. Reading and reflecting on the character of God and His ways, as revealed in Scripture,

b. Cultivating our personal, first hand knowledge of Him through prayer and communion with Him.

c. Being aware of, and observing His working in our life and in the lives of others.

4. Trust is not so much an act or a series of acts as a settled state of being.
Because it is based on a knowledge of God's character, trust is at rest in the face of an uncertain future or even when we cannot understand, or even misunderstand what God is doing. Trust leads to confidence and assurance in spite of baffling circumstances.

40

But blessed is the man who trusts in the Lord, whose confidence is in him. He will be like a tree planted by the water, that sends out its roots by the stream.

(Jeremiah 17:7)

Though he slay me, yet will I trust in him.

(Job 13:15, AV)

Though an army besiege me, my heart will not fear; though war break out against me, even then will I be confident.
(Psalm 27:3)

Being confident of this, that he who began a good work in you will carry it on to completion until the day of Jesus Christ.
(Philippians 1:6)

5. Trust has the confidence to wait for God.
Because of its knowledge of God, trust has the confidence to wait for his time to answer or to intervene, even when it means waiting in the dark without evidence or manifestation.

I will wait for the Lord who is hiding his face from the house of Jacob. I will put my trust in him. (Isaiah 8:17)

6. Trust's confident expectancy is very similar to hope.
Trust is oriented towards the future and because its object is God himself it has the expectancy of good things. Trust is therefore not passive but an active openness to receive.

A righteous man will be remembered forever. He will have no fear of bad news; his heart is steadfast, trusting the Lord. His heart is secure, he will have no fear; in the end he will look in triumph on his foes. (Psalm 112:6–8)

41

7. There is only one way to trust, that is with all your heart.
Because trust is essentially a matter of relationship based on knowledge of God, it is all or nothing, we trust with everything or we are not trusting.

> *Trust in the Lord with all your heart and lean not on your own understanding; in all your ways acknowledge him, and he will make your paths straight.*
>
> (Proverbs 3:5)

God trusts us

Trust as we have seen is an essential element of all relationships. It is therefore not strange that we are expected to trust God, just as we are to love him, to honour him and to know him.

What we need to realise however, is that God guards very jealously the integrity of our relationship with him. This means that he also abides by the categories that go to make up a relationship. He not only loves us (1 John 4:10), honours (values) us (Isaiah 43:4), and understands us (Hebrews 4:15), but he also trusts us.

> *So then men ought to regard us as servants of Christ, and as those entrusted with the secret things of God. Now it is required that those who have been given a trust must prove faithful.* (1 Corinthians 4:2–3)

The implications of this are staggering. God's trust is real trust. It is a choice he has made and it is a vulnerability that he has accepted. The vulnerability is that in order that we might experience the joy of being trusted by him, he has let some of the outcomes of his purposes go out of his sole control and shared them with us. What is more, it is real

42

trust, he has made no contingency plans in case we let him down.

That is why, in God's dealings with us, character is everything. His purpose is to conform us to the image (the character) of his Son (Romans 8:29), the One who *'is faithful as a son over God's house'* (Hebrews 3:6).

It is no surprise to find therefore, that in the early church, character ranked above everything else, above charism, above gift, above ministry.

> *And what you have heard from me before many witnesses entrust to faithful men who will be able to teach others also.* (2 Timothy 2:2, RSV)

God prizes faithfulness and trustworthiness because they reflect his own character, and because they are essential to us having a real relationship with him.

> *If we are faithless, he will remain faithful, for he cannot disown himself.* (2 Timothy 2:13)

6

Trust And Marriage

Trust lies at the very heart of marriage, in fact it permeates and is required at every stage and in every aspect of the relationship.

Trust and covenant

1. Marriage is a wide ranging symbol in scripture for the covenant relationship between God and his people, therefore the marriage relationship is covenantal in nature.

> *For your Maker is your husband, the Lord Almighty is his name, the Holy One of Israel is your Redeemer: he is called the God of all the earth.* (Isaiah 54:6)

In the new covenant Christ is the bridegroom (John 3:29) and the church is his bride (Revelation 21:9–10).

> *Let us rejoice and give him glory! For the wedding of the Lamb has come, and his bride has made herself ready.* (Revelation 19:7)

2. A covenant is a bond of personal loyalty between two parties, therefore the heart of the marriage covenant is the vows that the parties make towards one another. We say, 'This I vow before God.' By these vows we bind ourselves to

certain obligations and covenant requires that we be faithful to these vows and to the person to whom we made them.

To break these vows is to be unfaithful, that is to break troth, the solemn bond of fidelity and loyalty. The sin of adultery, is that it is covenant breaking.

3. The basis of the covenant between God and man is grace on his side and faith on our side. Thus also the relationships in the covenant of marriage consist of grace and faith.

Grace in human terms is simply doing good to one another with no strings attached. Grace is the prerequisite for trust and creates the climate within which trust is possible. It is not difficult to trust yourself to someone who lives towards you on the basis of doing you good with no strings attached.

Faith in human terms, as applied to marriage, is when two people join themselves to each other in a lifelong commitment, trusting each other for their,

1. Physical and material welfare and wellbeing
2. Spiritual health and wellbeing
3. Mental and emotional health and wellbeing
4. Sexual fulfilment and wellbeing
5. Social and relational fulfilment and wellbeing.

When we trust we let some of the outcomes of our life go out of our sole control and into the hands of the person we are trusting. The outcomes involved in marriage are among the most important, intimate and sensitive ones we have. Trusting these areas therefore creates great vulnerability which is why God has enclosed marriage within the security of covenant.

Trust and submission

The overriding principle that controls all Christian relationships is set out in Ephesians 5:21: '*Submit to one another out of reverence to Christ.*' What this means for the relationship

46

between husband and wife is expressed in the passage which follows,

> *Wives submit to your husbands as to the Lord. For the husband is head of the wife as Christ is head of the church, his body of which he is the Saviour.* (v 22)

> *Husbands love your wives just as Christ loved the church and gave himself up for her.* (v 25)

Note the following important points.

1. Submission involves trust because it is yielding certain rights to another. But the wife's submission is not unconditional because it is to be:

a. As to the Lord, and therefore only to what would be in harmony with his character and ways,

b. To a husband who lives towards her on the basis of grace, that is who loves and gives himself up for her in the same way as Christ loves and gives himself up for the church.

2. Trust creates responsibility, therefore the husband is responsible for and accountable for what is entrusted to him. This responsibility is in two directions:

a. As the head of his wife, he is responsible to his Head, that is to Christ Jesus the Lord.

b. He is also responsible to the one who has trusted him, that is, his wife, and accountable to her for what he has done with the trust placed in him.

Trust and sexual union

The categories of trust are specifically applied to the sexual union of marriage in 1 Corinthians 7. In trust, the outcome of some part of our life goes out of our sole control into the control of the person we are trusting. Paul says,

> *The wife's body does not belong to her alone but also to her husband. In the same way, the husband's body does not belong to him alone but also to his wife.*

(1 Corinthians 7:4)

Because trust necessitates trustworthiness, the giving of each other in sexual union in marriage is predicated on faithfulness.

Trust and openness

One of the most vital necessities to build trust in a marriage is walking in the light with one another, that is living in openness, sincerity and honesty. What inhibits trust is the knowledge of, or suspicion of hidden agendas, undisclosed secrets, and concealed or suppressed desires or motives. You cannot trust somebody you do not know, and you know a person only to the extent that they will reveal themselves to you.

But to walk openly with one another also requires trust because when all our secrets are out in the open we are at our most vulnerable. We have to trust therefore that our disclosures will be received fairly and compassionately, and that we will not be rejected because of what we reveal. Therefore openness generally develops gradually as husband and wife discover that it is safe to trust each other with secret fears and failings. And they make the discovery that vulnerability comes not through openness but through covering things up.

7

Trust And Leadership

In the relationship between leaders and people the most crucial element is probably trust. Generally you will find that the more important the relationship the more vital is the part played by trust.

All that has already been written applies to trust between people and leaders but note the following particular considerations that apply to leadership situations.

Leadership—a position of trust

Leadership is always a position of trust,

1. Superiors above the leaders may have entrusted them with the role or function of leadership and with it responsibility for results. One of the marks of a leader is that he is willing to shoulder responsibility.

2. The people who have committed themselves to the leaders or the leaders' goals have also trusted them, that is they have let major outcomes, or what they perceive as major outcomes, go out of their hands into the hands of the leaders.

Trust is therefore the cost of commitment and few leaders give sufficient attention to the cost of the trust they expect from their people almost as of right. Similarly, because they do not realise the emotional and psychological vulnerability involved, they are often dismayed at the anger and hostility that are directed towards them if they have been guilty of breach of trust.

Furthermore because leaders have more power and more information than others, they carry the greater burden of responsibility for the success of the relationship.

Trust and accountability

Trust brings responsibility and responsibility includes accountability. The question then is, 'To whom are leaders accountable or answerable?' The answer is 'To all those who have trusted them.'

That means that in the church, for example, leaders are accountable downwards as well as upwards. They are responsible to the people who follow them and have put their trust in them as leaders as well as to the superiors who may have appointed them to their position. They are answerable for the way they have led, because that is what people have trusted them to do.

What are people trusting in their leaders?

We must be clear as to what it is that people are trusting in their leaders. Either explicitly or implicitly it will be found to be the following elements.

1. The leaders' judgement
The task of leaders has to do with establishing the goals or objectives of the church or organisation. The people, because they cannot see the future as clearly as the leaders can, are trusting that the leaders have:

a. Got the goals right, that is they know what they are aiming for, and

b. Got the right goals, that is ones that are achievable with the resources available.

Note that they are trusting the leaders judgement, not their persuasiveness, therefore it is always more difficult to trust new or untried leaders because there is no track record to go on.

2. The leaders' resourcefulness

People are trusting the ability of the leaders to handle problems that may arise in the future and to overcome obstacles that stand in the way of reaching the objectives of the organisation.

Here again, confidence grows as leaders demonstrate their capacity to handle difficult situations, and particularly the ability to face problems without losing their nerve or moaning or complaining when things go wrong.

At other times, the people's confidence, or lack of confidence in their leaders is often a reflection of the leaders' self confidence, or lack of it. They cannot be sure of leaders who are not sure of themselves, and find difficulty in trusting the resourcefulness of leaders who are uncertain or indecisive.

3. The leaders' perseverence

People are trusting that their leaders will hang in there in the bad times as well as the good, until the goals are reached or the objectives achieved. Some leaders hand the reins over, or get a 'call' somewhere else if they think the venture is going to fail. They do not want their reputation tarnished by failures. If that attitude is in the leaders it will create deep uncertainty in the people even when things are going well.

Linked to perseverence is character, or moral fibre, that is the ability to stand up under pressure without buckling or giving way. Note the emphasis given to character in the leadership of the early church (1 Timothy 3:1–12, Titus 1:6–9, etc).

4. The leaders' integrity

As well as perseverence there are certain essential qualities of character that people look for in their leaders, including:

a. Honesty, so that their word can be relied on, the message is not dressed up differently for different people, or only part of the truth is told.

b. Fairness, that is, that leaders will be just and equitable in their treatment of people avoiding favouritism, partiality and discrimination.

c. Openness in admitting mistakes or errors of judgement without rationalising, making excuses or evading responsibility by 'passing the buck'. People will follow leaders almost anywhere as long as they have confidence that if the leaders make a mistake and get into danger they will admit it and lead them back into safety.

d. Confidentiality, so that sensitive matters entrusted to the leaders, or coming to the knowledge of the leaders, is in safe keeping.

e. Loyalty, that is that the leaders will stick by the people, support them and defend them against criticism or attack.

Leaders have to trust their people

Because of the mutuality of all relationships, that is, there has to be input from both sides, not only do people have to trust their leaders for the relationship to succeed, but leaders have to trust their people.

Because trust means letting certain outcomes go out of our sole control and at least partly into the control of others, it is temperamentally harder for leaders because they like to, and are accustomed to be in control. That is also why it is often difficult to lead leaders.

This lack of trust is often seen when leaders have difficulty in delegating responsibility and the power and authority that goes with responsibility. Similarly, when in a church or other organisation, leaders reserve to themselves the final authority in case things go wrong, the reason often is that at bottom they do not trust their people. Leaders who mistrust are no more likely to gain trust than leaders who are uncommitted are likely to gain commitment.

Breach of trust

When leaders fail in their leadership responsibilities there is also a breach of trust because people have trusted them to fulfil those functions. That is not to say that every mistake or error on the part of leaders constitutes a breach of trust, but some errors or blunders may be so serious, or repeated failures so inept that people lose confidence in their leadership capacity even when convinced of their sincerity.

There may be no moral blame attached to the foregoing failures, it may simply be that the leaders are out of their depth or lack experience, skill or training. But there may also be breaches of trust that involve moral blame or censure, as when leaders treat people unjustly or unfairly, or take advantage of their position for personal gain, or allow personal differences or conflicts among them to divide or weaken the church or organisation.

There is another important and often overlooked factor. When leaders are guilty of moral lapses or failures in their personal lives, there is, along with anything else, a breach of trust involved, because the leaders' private character cannot be separated from his public character.